PHILIP JOHNSTON
and the
NAVAJO CODE TALKERS

By
SYBLE LAGERQUIST

Council for Indian Education
2032 Woody Drive, Billings Montana 59102

1996 edition
Copyright 1975 by Syble Lagerquist

ISBN 8-9992-139-6

The Council for Indian Education

The Council for Indian Education is a non-profit organization devoted to teacher training and to the publication of materials to aide in the teaching of Native American children. All books published by the Council are selected and are approved for use with Indian children by a volunteer Intertribal Indian Editorial Board. Proceeds are used for the publication of more books for Native American children.

Editorial Board for
Philip Johnson and the Navajo Code Talkers

Hap Gilliland—Chairman
Marie Reyhner—Navajo
Rosalie BearCrane—Crow
Robert LaFountain—Chippewa
Elaine Allery—Chippewa-Cree
Rita McFadyean—Blackfeet-Cree
Joe Cooper—Yurok
William Spint—Crow
Gary Dollarhide—Cherokee
Mary Therese One Bear—Cheyenne
Julia Munoz Bradford—Hispanic-Lakota
Gail TallWhiteMan—Northern Cheyenne
Sharon Many Bead Bowers—Assiniboine-Haida
Heather Corson—Crow
Sally Old Coyote—Crow
Diane Bakun—Alaska
Delores Wing
Elizabeth Clark—Secretary of the Board
Jon Reyhner—Indian Education Specialist

MSU-B

*Two Navajo Code Talkers from World War II,
Carl N. Gorman and Samuel T. Holiday
with Philip Johnston.
Taken at a reunion of Fourth Marines
in Chicago June 1969.*

This was high country, a sort of plateau, more rugged and rocky than some of the land they'd crossed. There were bushes here and there, and a sort of gray grass growing.

Philip saw something on the far horizon. As the speck came closer and drew larger, he could see it was an Indian boy on a pony. Mr Johnston saw the rider coming and stopped the horses. He didn't need to say "Whoa." The horses were so tired they halted in their tracks at a slight pull on the reins.

Philip's father was a missionary. Mr. Johnston had been practicing a few Navajo words he felt he must know in order to communicate with the people he had come to help.

As the Indian boy stopped his horse beside the wagon, Philip's father tried out a few of his words. *"Hadi toh?"* he asked. This meant, "Where is water?"

"*Jo enlya tseh tseindi toh tohiui,*" came the quick reply.

The three pioneers listened, bewildered. They couldn't understand one word of the reply.

The Indian boy's eyes glittered with intelligence. He pointed the way, and

This was high country, a sort of plateau, more rugged and rocky than some of the land they'd crossed. There were bushes here and there, and a sort of gray grass growing.

Philip saw something on the far horizon. As the speck came closer and drew larger, he could see it was an Indian boy on a pony. Mr Johnston saw the rider coming and stopped the horses. He didn't need to say "Whoa." The horses were so tired they halted in their tracks at a slight pull on the reins.

Philip's father was a missionary. Mr. Johnston had been practicing a few Navajo words he felt he must know in order to communicate with the people he had come to help.

As the Indian boy stopped his horse beside the wagon, Philip's father tried out a few of his words. *"Hadi toh?"* he asked. This meant, "Where is water?"

"*Jo enlya tseh tseindi toh tohiui*," came the quick reply.

The three pioneers listened, bewildered. They couldn't understand one word of the reply.

The Indian boy's eyes glittered with intelligence. He pointed the way, and

waved them on. Riding ahead of the wagon, he sat straight and steady on his smooth brown pony, with only a rope around the animal's neck to guide him. Mr. Johnston straightened his own weary shoulders. Encouragement came back into his face, where sweat streaked the dust down his gaunt cheeks to his chin.

The boy rider led them to water—a spring at the foot of a cliff. He wore a dark blue velveteen shirt, which came down over the top of his white cotton pants with slits in the legs. His face glowed a soft warm brown. He sat on his horse serenely, and watched the people drink and water their horses. His long shiny black hair was tied at the back with string, the hair was rolled into a double loop and tied with more string. As the missionary family started to fill the casks on the wagon, the Indian rode off, and was lost over a hillock in the distance. He disappeared silently as if he had never been there at all.

The Johnstons travelled until dusk, when they stopped for the night. They cooked supper in the open, spreading their bedrolls under the wagon to sleep.

The next day they went on, and found a stone building that had been erected by an Englishman for a mill. The mill was not adaptable to the wool available, and hadn't worked out. The Johnstons found living space for a while in the abandoned building. Then came the getting acquainted, the learning and the teaching. Mr. Johnston soon found that even a bigger tasks than teaching the Navajos the white man's idea of God was the job of helping them with their problems.

Philip was soon talking with the Indian children in their own language, and interpreting for his father, who was trying to get the hang of the new words. The family built their second home of upright cottonwood lots on the bank of the Little Colorado River.

When Philip was nine years old, he went with his father and two of the old Indian leaders to Washington. Philip acted as interpreter between the Indians and President Theodore Roosevelt. The land upon which the Navajos were living was public domain. As a result of this meeting, President Roosevelt ordered the area withdrawn from sale and settlement. About three months later, he issued another executive order giving this land the status of a reservation, which is known today as the Leupp Extension.

By the time he was eleven, Philip was even doing his thinking in his adoped language. He knew nothing of slingshots, marbles, or baseball, but he did know he was lucky to be growing up in Navajo country. His games were *joh'l,* a kind of shinny, and other Indian fun. He was accurate with a bow and arrow, could use a lasso, and rode bareback, wild and free, on an Indian pony.

The names of the white boy's friends were not Jim or George or Jack. He played with Tsosi, Dilkoo, and Hozho.

He preferred moccasins to shoes.

Mutton roasted over an open fire was certainly better than meat fried in a skillet or baked in an oven. The *tocha*, or sweat bath, was far better than a bath in a galvanized tub. He looked upon the *pelakana*, or white man, as a foreigner. Philip Johnston thought of himself as a Navajo, even though the white family lived in a separate house as a separate family.

When Philip and his friend Nan'lkadi competed with bow and arrow, the Indian shouted, *"Nikanchosh!"* That meant "bugs in your arm." They both tried again, and hit the small stump at which they were shooting.

"Ashki hiui!" someone shouted, meaning "The boy is mighty." "Both *hiui*. Both will be great warriors."

The girls of the settlement washed their long black hair with suds made of pounded yucca root. They brushed it with a *bezho*, a brush made from stalks of grass tied with wool string, until it shone like silk. When

Navajo children herding sheep

girls dressed up in full calico skirts and blouses of colorful velveteen, they wore beads of turquoise, silver and coral.

The Navajo sheared their sheep and made the wool into yarn. This was dyed and woven into beautifully designed rugs and blankets. When sheep were killed for eating, the skins were pegged to the ground to dry. Hides from which the wool had been shorn were sold in the trading post. The cured hides with long fleece were laid on the hogan floor to sit upon and to be used as mattresses for sleeping.

In the camp of an Indian friend there was a big dog to guard the sheep. His name was _Yebitchi,_ meaning grandson of the giant. He was a whopper, and could keep the coyotes away from the little lambs. The Navajos said Yebitchi was _behotzit_ (dangerous) and they were to keep their distance from him.

The big yellow dog sat so still, and seemed so tame, Philip walked up to the creature. As he put out his hand to pet the beast, Yebitchi exploded into snarling action. The next thing Philip knew, he was on the ground. There was a three-inch gash in his head, open to the skull, and there was shouting and beating of clubs as the snarling dog was driven off.

The house in the left side of this picture is Philip's boyhood home on the reservation.

Philip's father sewed up the wound with needle and thread from his mother's sewing basket, and doused it with strong antiseptic. It was said after that that Yebitchi was <u>chendi</u> (a devil).

The Indian boys and Philip made balls for their shinny games out of tough cloth packed tightly with wool. The ball was two and a half inches in diameter. The clubs were made of *dowuzhi,* or greasewood. The sticks were nearly three feet long. The end was curved by soaking in water and bending between hot stones, over and over, until it took on a "L" shape. The games were rough, injuries many. All the players on both sides were Indians except Philip.

Thus Philip Johnston grew up with the Navajos. When he was older, his family moved to Los Angeles, California, where Philip went to college. He graduated from USC and became a civil engineer. He fought with the Army in World War I.

PART II

THE NAVAJO CODE TALKERS

Learning the Navajo language was perhaps the most important event of Philip Johnston's childhood. This was the key to something he did when he grew up, which was of great value to his country, and brought belated recognition to his Indian friends.

It was many years after his service in the Army in World War I that this second opportunity came. Although he had kept in touch with the Indians, and helped with their problems, all these years, the events of another war brought them closer as they again joined forces with a single purpose.

During World War II, Philip Johnston was very concerned about our military setbacks, so often due to communications leaks. Codes were broken almost as fast as they were worked out. A code over 24-hours old was considered of no use.

In the early 1940's Philip was working for the City of Los Angeles as a civil engineer. His office was like a prison: his slide rule, a ball and chain. He wanted to do something for the war effort—but what?

At night he paced the floor, thinking, thinking. All the time his mind kept going back to his childhood among the Navajos, and to the language he'd learned as a child. Very few people in the world, outside the Navajo Nation could understand that language. Why couldn't a code be worked out using Navajo men who could talk to each other by radio in a code made up of Navajo words? Philip knew lots of smart young Navajos capable of learning and practicing a code. Philip, himself, was too old for the draft, too old for enlistment, really. He'd served his country well, but he wanted to do more.

No one would listen to him when he told them they could make an unbreakable doce for military use. It couldn't be done, they said. Philip's pacing became more angry. There must be someone who would listen. He had this one more thing to offer his country—and there were no takers.

War talk went on—of stolen codes: new codes broken overnight; military secrets made available to the enemy like sand in an hourglass running out. Why wouldn't they try Philip Johnston's code idea? He knew from experience you had to grow up with the Navajo language to speak it properly. It was practically unwritable. This would have to be an oral code.

He talked with communications officers at a Marine Camp in San Diego. They didn't think the idea would work, but said he could bring some Navajo friends down from Los Angeles for a demonstration.

At his own expense, Philip Johnston took four young Navajos to San Diego.

*Philip Johnston, Staff Sgt. USMC
when he was training Navajo Code Talkers
1942-44*

They were given forty-five minutes to translate six military messages into Navajo. In these messages were many terms for which there were no equivalents in the Navajo language. Philip Johnston and his Navajo friends devised simple translations on the spot. They then demonstrated this "hurry-up code" from English to Navajo and back to English again, to show General Clayton B. Vogel and his staff that a Navajo-English code was possible.

The officers were not about to believe there could be such a thing as an unbreakable code. As the demonstration went on, they were amazed, and then convinced. A message was given to a Navajo in English, either written or verbal. The Indian transmitted the message in his native tongue, and another Navajo in a distant room heard the radio message, and gave it back in English.

Largely because of this demonstration,

the Marine Corps inducted twenty-nine Navajos as Communications Specialists in February, 1942. After boot camp, four of these Navajos devised the Navajo Code.

The Code worked well in combat, so 300 additional Navajos were inducted. In the fall of 1942, the Marine Corps enlisted Philip Johnston with a waiver, because of his age, to help recruit and train these men. These young men were sent to boot camp after recruitment, then turned over to Staff Sergeant Johnston for training in the use of the code. Then, in early 1943, Philip worked with the professional code makers in developing a more sophisticated code.

Besides working out each letter of the alphabet, so difficult words could be spelled out, the code makers worked up names for military expressions which have no equivalent in the Navajo tongue. The way the code was set up, even an untrained Navajo who knew the language couldn't make out what was being said. They had a secret way of telling when they were going to spell things out. A̱nt, Ḇear, C̱at in Navajo became A, B, C in code.

Besides the alphabet words, they learned the 413 code names in a word list. Intelligent, quick to learn, the Indians became very good. There were no Navajo words for most military terms. An oral code was made, using Navajo sounds for English words. Chicken hawk in Navajo meant dive bomber; hummingbird, a fighter plane; iron fish, a submarine. Fast shooter was used for machine gun. Iron rain meant a barrage.

From Guadalcanal to the last battle in the Pacific, the code was never broken. This was the only code used by the Marine Corps at Iwo Jima.

One incident tells of our fighters being barraged by their own men. "Raise your sights," the radioed in another code. "You're hitting us."

"Sorry," the answer came back, "your

Philip Johnston wearing the medallion presented at the reunion of Fourth Marines, Summer 1969.

secret way of telling when they were going to spell things out. A̲nt, B̲ear, C̲at in Navajo became A, B, C in code.

Besides the alphabet words, they learned the 413 code names in a word list. Intelligent, quick to learn, the Indians became very good. There were no Navajo words for most military terms. An oral code was made, using Navajo sounds for English words. Chicken hawk in Navajo meant dive bomber; hummingbird, a fighter plane; iron fish, a submarine. Fast shooter was used for machine gun. Iron rain meant a barrage.

From Guadalcanal to the last battle in the Pacific, the code was never broken. This was the only code used by the Marine Corps at Iwo Jima.

One incident tells of our fighters being barraged by their own men. "Raise your sights," the radioed in another code. "You're hitting us."

"Sorry," the answer came back, "your

Philip Johnston wearing the medallion presented at the reunion of Fourth Marines, Summer 1969.

PART III
A HISTORICAL NOTE

History books tell of the long bitter battles of the Pacific, the taking of one island after another, and the triumph at Iwo Jima. Battles were shortened, were turned to victory, aided by the unbreakable code Philip Johnston helped create. The flag raising at Suribachi was the clincher when Navajo Code Talkers put that name over the air.

Military men have said the use of the Navajo Code Talkers didn't shorten the war—the A bomb did that. BUT, by that time all of the places overrun by the Japanese forces had been reconquered.

In 1969, when the Fourth Marines held their 22nd reunion in Chicago, Philip Johnston and a number of Code Talkers still alive were invited to the meetings. A big event of the reunion was the tribute

Philip Johnston in 1970

paid to Code Talkers who could be found. They were given bronze medallions showing an Indian on a pony in the foreground, and the Iwo Jima Flag-raising in the background. The medallions were hung from rawhide thongs, strung with red, white and blue Indian beads. President Nixon sent his personal representative to present the awards and to read a message from the Chief Executive. As a climax, Philip Johnston sang the Marine Corps Hymn—in NAVAJO!

The Navajo Code Talkers held a reunion in 1971 at their own stomping grounds near Window Rock, Arizona. They astounded the younger generation, as well as old timers, with their still keen ability to send and receive coded messages. It was a grand and exciting day. And Philip Johnston was there.

His Navajo friends remember Philip Johnston as one of those who kept prodding until the Government took action to improve the educational and living conditions of the Indians. Most of his eighty years have been spent in assisting the Navajos in every way he could. Now he watches with pride as young men of the Navajo Nation take hold of their own destinies.